I0486886

A Way To Wealth –
The Art of Investing in Common Stocks

By
John R. Reizner

Dedication

To My Family,
Who were there when the need was greatest.
And to Nora,
Whose great example and love inspire me.

Library of Congress Control Number: 2007908031
Publisher: BookSurge Publishing
North Charleston, South Carolina

Contents

Disclosure

The Graphs, "Guide to Using Daily Graphs" and "Explanation Of The Fundamental and Technical Features of Daily Graphs" reproduced in the following pages are excerpted from the pages of Daily Graphs® a William O'Neil + Company Incorporated publication.

William O'Neil + Company is also the producer of the Daily Graphs Online® products available at *www.dailygraphs.com.*

I have used Daily Graphs along with other sources for over twenty years to research and select stocks for my personal investments. It has proved to be an excellent provider of information salient to my investment process. All of the stocks described in this report have been researched in part or wholly through the publication, and a major part of my investment process is derived through interpretation of information contained in *Daily Graphs.*

John R. Reizner

Outstanding Investor Digest, or *OID*, has been an important and valuable addition to my investment process. Specifically, the publication's interviews with fine investors influenced my decision to buy shares of Wells Fargo in the early 1990's, when the bank was widely perceived to be on its knees. In 1992, in the pages of *OID*, Bruce Berkowitz powerfully illustrated the case for buying Wells Fargo, demonstrating its underlying earnings power. Having considered his arguments as well as other research, I purchased shares, and have seen them multiply many times in value in the years since.

OID is no one-hit wonder. It has continued over the years to interview many of the country's best investment managers, always providing investors with jewels of information to help them win the investment war. *Outstanding Investor Digest* can be located on the Web at http://www.oid.com and at 295 Greenwich Street, Box 282, New York, NY 10007.

John R. Reizner   v

LIMIT OF LIABILITY AND DISCLAIMER OF WARRANTY: THIS WORK CONTAINS THE OPINIONS AND IDEAS OF ITS AUTHOR AND IS DESIGNED TO PROVIDE USEFUL INFORMATION TO THE READER ON THE SUBJECT MATTER COVERED. THE AUTHOR MAY OR MAY NOT HAVE CURRENT POSITIONS IN THE INVESTMENTS MENTIONED IN THIS WORK, AND THE AUTHOR MAY FROM TIME TO TIME MAKE INVESTMENTS IN A MANNER THAT IS NOT DESCRIBED HERE. PAST PERFORMANCE IS NO GUARANTEE OR PREDICTION OF FUTURE RESULTS AND ANY INVESTMENTS MADE BASED ON THE OPINIONS AND IDEAS CONTAINED IN THIS WORK MAY OR MAY NOT BE SUCCESSFUL. THE PUBLISHER AND THE AUTHOR MAKE NO REPRESENTATIONS, GUARANTEES, PREDICTIONS OR WARRANTIES WITH RESPECT TO THE ACCURACY OR COMPLETENESS OF THE CONTENTS OF THIS WORK AND SPECIFICALLY DISCLAIM ALL WARRANTIES, INCLUDING WITHOUT LIMITATION WARRANTIES OF FITNESS FOR A PARTICULAR PURPOSE. NO WARRANTY MAY BE CREATED OR EXTENDED BY SALES OR PROMOTIONAL MATERIALS. THE ADVICE AND STRATEGIES CONTAINED HEREIN MAY NOT BE SUITABLE FOR EVERY SITUATION. THIS WORK IS SOLD WITH THE UNDERSTANDING THAT NEITHER THE PUBLISHER NOR THE AUTHOR IS ENGAGED IN RENDERING LEGAL, ACCOUNTING, INVESTMENT ADVISORY OR OTHER PROFESSIONAL SERVICES. IF PROFESSIONAL ASSISTANCE IS REQUIRED, THE SERVICES OF A COMPETENT PROFESSIONAL SHOULD BE SOUGHT. NEITHER THE PUBLISHER NOR THE AUTHOR SHALL BE LIABLE FOR DAMAGES, LOSSES OR RISK THAT MAY BE CLAIMED OR INCURRED AS A CONSEQUENCE, DIRECTLY OR INDIRECTLY, OF THE USE AND/OR APPLICATION OF THE CONTENTS OF THIS WORK. THE FACT THAT AN ORGANIZATION OR WEBSITE IS REFERRED TO IN THIS WORK AS A CITATION AND/OR A POTENTIAL SOURCE OF FURTHER INFORMATION DOES NOT MEAN THAT THE AUTHOR OR THE PUBLISHER ENDORSES THE INFORMATION THE ORGANIZATION OR WEBSITE MAY PROVIDE OR RECOMMENDATIONS IT MAY MAKE. FURTHER, READERS SHOULD BE AWARE THAT INTERNET WEBSITES LISTED IN THIS WORK MAY HAVE CHANGED OR DISAPPEARED BETWEEN WHEN THIS WORK WAS WRITTEN AND WHEN IT IS READ.

LEGAL_US_W # 53333317.3

Foreword

In the field of equities, an "insider" in general is either a company officer, director or an owner of at least 10% of a public company's shares.

Many people understand the term "insider trading" to mean a purely illegal form of owning stocks, akin to the charges against Martha Stewart. It is true that it is illegal to buy or sell the stock of a company if one is in possession of material, non-public information about that company. For example, if I were tipped by an officer of a pharmaceutical company that one of the firm's drugs will be approved for sale, and then I acted on that information by buying shares of the company prior to the news being disclosed publicly, I would be violating the law.

Legal insider trading occurs when corporate insiders buy or sell shares of their company and report that activity to the SEC within two days. If I take note of the publicly-reported behavior of insiders as reported in publications such as *Daily Graphs*, and make investing decisions based on their behavior, my actions would be entirely legal.

There is widespread, continuing discussion and research in financial periodicals, television, etc. about the meaning of legal insider trading in choosing worthwhile stocks for investment. I believe that a person's success in choosing stocks can be significantly improved by a careful study of open market insider purchases, combined with other knowledge as described in this book. In the book, I provide comprehensive examples of how I analyzed insiders' open market purchases to use in order to profit from my investments.

John R. Reizner

Introduction

From the late 1970's through the present day, I have been and am the originator and developer of a successful systematic method of investing in common stocks and equity mutual funds. I have tested this method for over a decade with my personal assets. With reasonable diversification, it has grown my net worth in good times, and preserved much of it in very challenging markets. I achieved much of this as a Wall Street outsider, as part of the investing public, *not* as a securities analyst, portfolio manager, or investment banker.

This is *not* a traditional scientific study, but rather a description of an investment process, which really boils down to a dynamic state of mind, which I illustrate using specific examples of how I invested my personal funds in all kinds of markets.

I will attempt in this description of my method to explain the process. In the examples and experiences I describe, I will include the investing environment of the time, the rules to which I adhered, and my experience as I interacted with the events and knowledge out there. I will describe what I learned from others, revealing both a very workable investment process as well as my personal results. I believe these results compare well with those of many Wall Street professionals offering their services to the public.

Let me tell you that I am not among the wealthiest of market investors. But neither am I remotely close to being among the poorest. In my life, I have certainly learned the value of reasonably spreading the risk in my stock selections. For many years, my primary income and the source of my investment capital have come from my investments in individual stocks, mutual funds, treasuries and bank accounts. I have survived the battle with my wits and money about me, at least so far.

In this work, I will sometimes refer to the methods of those investors whom I call "seers" or visionaries in their field: those who, based on their long experience, can "see" what is usually the right thing to do at the right time. Often, this means going against prevailing Wall Street opinions, various buy lists, or model portfolios. These visionaries are men and women such as the late Edson Gould, the very present Warren Buffett, and John Templeton. I am a peon compared to these men but, in this tome, I will add to the greater body of knowledge my own understanding and experience, complete with examples, insights and rules, and demonstrate my techniques.

This investment process involves getting the right publications, including sources such as *Daily Graphs* and *Outstanding Investor Digest*. It also means reading the volumes that many successful investors write, such as Peter Lynch's popular writings.

Armed with data from *Daily Graphs*, you will be able to see when and how corporate insider buying is conducted by company officers. These are entirely legal purchases of company stock made by the people who run the company, who must, by law, report their buys and sells to the proper government agency. Company insiders are required to report their purchases within two days after execution to the SEC.

Investments made with their own hard cash in the open market are the most important kind, which *Daily Graphs* filters. They are completely different from illegal "insider trading," where top officers and/or their associates act on non-public information and buy company stock based on that undisclosed information. This all means, under particular circumstances that will become clear, that you will be able to buy as company officers do when they make "legal" insider trades — and at much better prices than you'll get by following the advice of typical Wall Street brokerage research reports. By noting the buying behavior of the best equity managers in the country, keeping price-earnings ratios down, and understanding such macro issues such as general market trends and Federal Reserve policy, you will have that elusive edge over many professionals.

Knowledge is a beautiful thing. Developing your knowledge of the stock market and insight into how the players interact with the information that is out there is a worthy calling. As a member of the public, I believe you can be a stock market winner and survive in the investment battle.

John R. Reizner

A Way To Wealth

Some have argued that there is an unspoken code, a cipher that unlocks unending profits in the stock market. I think that exists in the mind and experience of the beholder. Individuals may, according to their know-how and experience in the world of investments, and if they are lucky to live long enough, gain a key to the kingdom. One person's education and ability to learn from doing just may lead to the development of a number of successful processes for investing in equities.

In the process I have developed, one of the primary filters for making the decision to buy a given stock is the top officers', known as insiders, purchase of their company stock. They do this with their own hard cash in the open market in order to make money for themselves. *My research shows that it is essential to identify when such insider buys are made in succeeding or alternate weeks, and at what given price range. Concentrations of insider purchases can be the main stepping stone, often combined with further research, in finding stocks for purchase.*

Knowledge in this vein can be money: success depends upon the ability to have a vision of realistic possible outcomes and acting on that likely outcome. When an individual such as Warren Buffett, John Neff, or another "seer" with long experience, is buying, *and* there is qualifying insider buying, take notice. That can be the time to step up to the plate. The odds are with you. Investors such as those masters, together with the people running the company, know how to calculate value. *I call this type of purchase one made with confirmation. The smart, often contrarian, money is betting on a likely future outcome of a much higher stock price. And much more often than not, they are right.* All that is often needed is the confluence of these two factors. At the time, the mood about the company may be, as we will see, quite dark and controversial. Then you can feel good about bucking the crowd and actually buy a company under stress, or one operating in a challenging time for its business, or for the market in general. There are further conditions applying to this investment process that will become clear a bit later.

Multiples of
My Investment

The early 1990's were a time of brief wartime conflict and recession. Yet, one of my better macro indicators, the direction of the discount rate, was extremely bullish. Federal Reserve Chairman Alan Greenspan had begun lowering the discount rate and reserve requirements in response to the deepening banking crisis and real estate depression. As it later turned out, many banks affected by the downturn were actually selling at bargain prices. The more resilient banks' share prices were falling sharply along with banks which were outright failing. Thus one could have picked up the quality banks at good prices at that time.

During those days, I was looking for redemption in the pages of my weekly NYSE edition of *Daily Graphs*. I noticed that there were *successive insider purchases of Wells Fargo stock* in the 60's. The unadjusted price today would amount to about $750 per share. As it turned out, around then, my issue of *Outstanding Investor Digest* arrived in the mail. There were lengthy salient interviews with some who, in my mind, were visionary players. Bruce Berkowitz, for example, was quite positive on Wells Fargo stock at the time, a remarkably controversial opinion then.

The interview with Berkowitz was filled with reasons why Wells management *was* different from the other banks that had gone bust. He stated, "Wells Fargo has had fantastic earnings in the past. I don't see any reason it won't continue. In fact it's growing. Its earnings power has been disguised by the intense provisioning for loan losses. But when the provisioning gets back to a normal level, you'll start to see that incredible earning power come down to the bottom line. And it's as simple as that. The recession will end one day. And when it does, Wells will make a fortune. "[1]

There were also a huge number of short sellers who were depressing the stock price. Some of these vocal players contended that the bank might actually fail. They said that management's acclaimed pricing of their real estate loans was no better than many other banks' that had fallen on hard times. Should I purchase Wells Fargo stock, I would have to steel myself and go against the shorts. Adding to my process, it was a California bank, where the real estate depression was acute.

Yet for me, the picture was in process. I had read and reread the interviews, and had the benefit of solid insider support of my selection. And shorts, when they are wrong, can propel the stock upward should there be a squeeze. I calmly called my bank officer, and requested he buy Wells Fargo for my account. The chat was more than ten years ago, but I still remember the three words I heard coming through the phone: "California real estate!" The officer was hemming and hawing. He honestly didn't want me to get hurt. The buy was too risky and it would be better for me to be comfortable and do nothing, or buy another stock.

---

[1] See *Bruce Berkowitz, Lehman Brothers* (Conversations with OID) Outstanding Investor Digest (November 25, 1992) page 64.

And with that utterance from my bank officer, "California real estate," I did not buy the stock, at least not yet. Every Sunday, I perused my copy of *Daily Graphs*. Then, the stock rose into the 70's, and my unbacked selection had only begun its upward path. It does not often happen this way, but in the 70's, there was *more* qualifying insider buying.

I was resolved. I telephoned my bank with the intention of buying shares, a lesser amount than at the time of my previous call. I firmly told the bank over the wire to buy shares of Wells Fargo for my account. It was done. I had my stock and would bear witness to its multiyear ascent.

Initially, not surprisingly, the stock price was under a bit of pressure. But later, during earnings season, I was watching financial television when the Wells Fargo number was broadcast.

I heard the number. I was in heaven! They beat the consensus by a slim penny, and the stock vaulted into the 90's! I felt fortunate and vindicated.

Not a testament to my character then, I called my bank officer. Cackling nonsense into the phone, I'm sure I sounded strange, as I enjoyed getting my digs in. After all, I had shown the pro a thing or two.

In the time after the earnings announcement, Wells vaulted past 100. But then a reaction drove the shares back into the low 90's. I bought an additional small number of shares, satisfying an emotional desire to make up for the lower number I bought in the first place. After all, I was still young. A bit later, the bank suggested I take a short-term profit on part of my position, as I would participate on any upside move on the remainder. I refused, and held onto my stock. Shortly afterward, I removed the bank as co-manager of my account, and switched it over to a (bookkeeping) account.

In time, Wells Fargo reached the 130's. Then I saw a news blip in the Wells Fargo graph in *Daily Graphs:* the philanthropist Walter Annenberg was buying stock in the 130's. I increased my position slightly without, unfortunately, the support of company insiders. The calendar turned and in time I sold a small number of shares around the 310's. Wells has since done even better. When the bank merged with Norwest, but kept the Wells Fargo name, an effective 15-1 split took place. I sold a greater number of shares at pre-split 675 for purposes of reasonable diversification. The stock price now post-split is about $57 per share. I had made good money on this one while still honing my skills, and by and large sticking to method, without listening to the drum of Wall Street house and bank research.

Johnson & Johnson

There was great controversy after the 1992 election, when Hillary Clinton was put in charge of forming a new nationalized healthcare system. In fact, this would have resulted in a severe restraint in research and developments of new drugs, medical equipment, and techniques: the incentives for research and development simply wouldn't be there. It might eventually be unprofitable to invest in these activities because of government price cutbacks. Further, my own doctor pointed out that it could actually be illegal for me to be his patient should the scheme become law. Instead, some regional bureaucracy would assign a doctor to me. That's not to say, of course, that we shouldn't have a safety net for the uninsured.

During this time of furious debate, stock prices of drug firms possibly affected by an unfavorable outcome were plunging. *I identified insider buying in only one of these stocks, Johnson & Johnson.* The climate was dark. Yet, simultaneously, Johnson & Johnson insiders were buying their firm's shares in the open market. I steeled myself and purchased a small position for my account. It was a pure contrarian play at the time and, since my buy, the stock has risen fivefold.

At the time of my purchase, however, there was the clear risk that the industry would be regulated and dynamic growing employers stifled, with a decline in profits and company stock prices. So, not surprisingly, initially after my buy, the stock price fell more than 25%. Even my banker said the only good drug firm was Schering Plough. Then a friend, who had tuned into a popular weekly financial TV program, told me that both John Templeton and Peter Lynch had expressed their own very positive views on Johnson & Johnson. Not too long after, the stock turned upward and began its multi-year climb, and split 2-1 twice over the years. In late 1999, I sold one-fifth of my stake. Happy days.

I would like to take a moment to say that no stock is immune to a serious decline in price, either due to circumstances specific to the company or relative to a bear market. Yet, as I will demonstrate, there is ample opportunity to make money in both bull and bear phases. In a strong bull market, it is quite possible, as we have seen, to earn multiples of one's investment. In a bear trend, holding periods shorten, transaction costs go up, and the return is much less. I do not recommend selling short.

Recognizing the onset of a bear market is easier said than done, so I have my own personal roster of wise market commentators to whom I pay attention on this front. Practicing the method as told in this volume does not require a general market opinion.

Also, I advise placing a healthy portion of your investment funds into well-managed value or deep value mutual funds for the long haul. (Yes, there are still a handful.) This will play a significant role in assuring your continued wealth over time. There is more about all this in my sections on bear market investing, mutual funds, money management, and macro indicators.

MBIA

In December 1994, news arrived that Bob Citron, the treasurer of Orange County, California, was responsible for a $1.6 billion dollar dent in the county's capital. Citron had been speculating that interest rates would decline with county funds in complex derivatives, and his huge wager backfired. Orange County was then forced to declare bankruptcy, a real blow to this bastion of conservatism.

Ramifications shook through the related markets. MBIA, a NYSE-listed guarantor of municipal bonds, was rumored to be a casualty of the bankruptcy through the default of the county's bonds. The stock fell sharply.

My research indicated that the MBIA portfolio would not in this case be terribly affected, and that the plunge in the company's stock price was temporary and unwarranted. Further, both a respected value fund manager and company insiders were picking up shares in a manner that drew my attention. I stepped up to the plate and bought shares that have more than tripled since. Along the way, I did sell one-fifth of my position in order to maintain a moderate diversification of my holdings.

Recently, the company was in the news as short sellers were depressing the price, but the stock and earnings have recovered nicely from this bout. Insiders are not picking up shares at this time.

John R. Reizner **13**

John R. Reizner

Stock Investment
in a Declining Market

I will illustrate my stock investment in one of the most severe bear markets in a long while: the bear market phase from 2000 to late 2002.

Purchases made during this decline, but now profitably closed out are Tenet Healthcare (before it became a fallen angel), Family Dollar Stores and Deluxe Corp. Household International (now HSBC) almost doubled in price after my purchase, but I did not take advantage of the higher price to sell and am now about even.

Tenet Healthcare

In July and August of 1999, Tenet Healthcare's stock price was suffering. It roamed between 16 and 18 dollars per share, down from its high of 40 in 1998. Yet during this two-month period, *company insiders picked up shares for six consecutive weeks.* I did not make my move until late November because of illness, when I bought shares around 21. On the same day, I entered a "good till canceled" order above the market to sell at 33 or better. Frankly, neither I nor my broker thought it would reach that point, as the stock was languishing. Yet, as often is the case when insiders put their money on their vision of the company's true value, the firm's fortunes improved and the stock price executed a remarkable turnaround. It took until the fourth quarter of 2001, when I was indeed out at 33. But even there, the company became a Wall Street favorite, appearing on some buy lists and in some mutual funds. The stock reached more than 60. Then, in late 2002, bad news cratered the stock below 20, where it had begun its prior move.

This example of bear market investing yielded about 50%.

Deluxe Corporation

Deluxe Corp. is familiar to many people as the provider of printed checks. It is a seasoned company and pays a hefty dividend, yet its price in late 2000 was less than $20 per share as the general market's fall took down most equities. *The outlook for Deluxe must have been getting better, as insiders accumulated shares just below 20, and again between 20 and 25.* The price was more than 30 before it came to my attention. In 2000, we were in a bad market, and *insiders were still buying for their accounts.* At this higher level, I thought I could get roughly 48 for the stock, approximately double the average price insiders paid. I punched down for my account at about $35 per share.

Deluxe continued to climb to 50 in a fairly rapid ascent even while under the pressure of some sharp insider selling. After the stock hit 50, it rolled over and sank back down to 35. Then, about one year after my purchase, the price popped up to 45, where I took profits and sold out.

As a point of note, the reason that Deluxe's stock price fell sharply after its advance to 50, was that it was known that the next earnings report would be flat compared to the same quarter a year ago. With this in the background, Deluxe would be "dead money" for a while, though the dividend offered price support. Remember also that this was an unforgiving market, with poor business conditions, and one had to protect against possible further erosion in the stock price.

It is important to note that insider selling in general is not as meaningful as insider buying, unless it persists weekly for many months at a higher price plateau. When that happens, insider selling may portend a worse future for both the company and its stock. Enron, as an example, demonstrated insider selling at lofty levels for months before it began its descent into bankruptcy.

Family Dollar Stores and Moody's

As the end of 1999 marked the topping of an aging bull and unfolded into the first half of 2000, I took notes that there were *two alternate weeks of insider buying* at around 15 of Family Dollar Stores. This company is a discount retailer of items priced less than $10. Quarterly earnings were growing respectably, but the general market's decline had taken a toll on the firm's share price.

I decided to barely tip my toe into the water and purchased a small amount at about $18 per share. As events unfolded and the retail group came into favor on the Street, the stock price advanced to 30 by August 2001. Then the market was pounded by the terrible events of 9/11. The stock fell below 24, but then later advanced to over 35. I sold my shares, for a reasonable bear market profit of 80%.

During the bear phase, it was made known that Warren Buffett was buying Dun and Bradstreet, which later spun off Moody's Corp. It was also the case that insiders were picking up shares in a manner that qualified for my methodology, and so I bought shares. Later during this bear, I sold out my position for double my cost, as that was my parameter for what I thought I could achieve in an extended difficult market.

Missteps in a Bear Market

Sometimes, there is no telling how low is low for bear markets, as it is true that bull markets can surprise and confound skeptics on the upside. My mistake in the 2000-2002 bear consisted of not translating the downturn in technology stocks (in which I rarely invest directly) into big board stocks. Again, this error did not get in the way of my practicing the method described in this volume, but here are two that did not work out.

As the millennium bear unfolded, Warren Buffett also bought such issues such as Great Lakes Chemical and USG. I purchased both company's stocks after identifying insider buys. I got trounced on USG, as widespread asbestos lawsuits drove the shares down. I sold those shares, as well as my shares of Great Lakes Chemical, as the latter was not responding and I wanted to reallocate the funds. I would like to say that Warren Buffett's purchase of Moody's, as referenced above, was a much larger "bet" for him than represented by his purchase of the GLK and USG. The lesson learned is that Mr. Buffett's larger purchases may have a better risk profile in general, and the smaller investor observing his behavior should think accordingly.

My medium term trades in Sears, JP Morgan, and General Electric were not missteps as much as they were cases of somewhat premature selling after I had realized excellent percentage profits. I recently held Blockbuster Entertainment, which exhibited a great frequency of insider buys, but was sold at a loss. Other recent purchases are PNC Financial, Anheuser Busch and Wal-Mart, all of which exhibited good insider buying activity and reasonable price-earnings ratios. Anheuser Busch has the added advantage of being a Warren Buffett bet and so I allocated extra funds in this position. I sold Wal-Mart as I anticipated the possibility of a significant stock price decline, and I wished to deploy those funds elsewhere.

My Insider Buying Rules

♦ Valid buy signals consist of open market buying as shown in Daily Graphs in two or more consecutive or alternate weeks. Simultaneous insider *selling*, for both above references, or a week of insider selling in between insider buy weeks (for alternate buy weeks), remove the candidate for consideration.

♦ Do not buy candidates priced under $10 per share.

♦ Eliminate yesterday's high fliers that have fallen on hard times.

♦ Simply do not buy technology stocks. I have not studied tech stocks thoroughly, but they are more unpredictable in my view. Many of these are less seasoned companies, and it is often impossible to predict the winners five or ten years hence.

♦ Stick mainly to NYSE established companies. My research doesn't extend to the NASDAQ. I've always experienced and believed that pricing is much fairer on the Big Board and, I think many on Wall Street may agree with that.

♦ Don't let prevailing Wall Street research influence you. A series of strong buy ratings on your stock could indicate an opportunity to sell on strength. It pays to lean against the prevailing opinion.

♦ Be aware that your stock could easily trade below your cost for weeks or months before its likely recovery. If there is insider selling below the insider's own buy level, as reported in *Daily Graphs*, then it is time to reevaluate whether to hold on or to sell your position. Ask yourself how the stock's current price-earnings ratio and dividend yield compare to its longer-term history.

♦ One can buy stock that is experiencing insider buying without having a visionary such as Warren Buffett also buying. However, my experience indicates that one should not buy a visionary's selection without the company insiders also putting their funds at risk.

♦ Keep the price-earnings ratio of your selections at approximately 15 or less when you buy them.

♦ The world is dynamic and ever changing. It is not in stasis. Events and outlooks constantly change, and that includes your stock research, the companies, and their share prices.

Mutual Fund Investing for Wealth

Equity mutual funds can provide, at their best, steady, long-term growth of one's wealth. I believe the key to profits in this area, is *to find funds less likely to lose back a large part of their gains in a difficult market.* This end is compatible with long-term growth of capital achieved in bull markets. This means staying away from the investment fad of the moment, the currently "hot" funds, and instead, I believe, choosing value type managers. Well-chosen funds of this sort can and do provide reasonable growth, as they do not overpay for stocks in euphoric markets. Rather, the manager attempts to find bargains, and sells them when their stocks' prices are marked up to full value by the market. Value investing, and there are variations of this method, is a solid, time-tested way to achieve your financial goals.

Before you invest in any fund, you should read the fund's prospectus, including looking at the fund's goals and expense ratio. Also, look at a semi-annual or annual report of the fund, which should contain a list of all the portfolio's investments. If these are your sort of investments, and you are happy with the comments and prowess of the manager, then consider further. Before investing, you may want to telephone the fund representatives or the manager or check online in order to discover more about their philosophy, practices, and investments.

Do not invest in a fund that has been around for less than four or five years, unless it is from a fund family you can trust. In any event, pay attention to the manager's track record, noting how well the investments hold up in a down market. There are also helpful publications out there, including *Forbes* magazine, which publishes a very good grading of the fund universe, with performance ratings for both good and bad markets.

When you find yourself in a good, well-managed fund, there is a strong incentive to hold onto the fund as long as possible. Should you need money, consider selling just a portion of your holding. Attempt not to sell unless the long-term fund performance has been compromised. Be patient. Don't expect to make huge gains overnight and, if you do, ask yourself and the fund's representatives how they will sustain the gains. Slow and steady are usually the watchwords here. Personally, I have never lost money in a mutual fund.

Money Management

There is an old racetrack saying: "Scared money never wins." If losing your next bet or two is going to break you, then you shouldn't be making it in the first place. There is much to be said for having both a real and psychological cushion created by a core of assets at your disposal and wisely invested to foster better risk-taking and better sleep.

Through the years, when risking money to make money on individual stocks, I frequently place between 3/4 to 2% of my portfolio in each company. I have put up to 1 to 2% of my portfolio in each of my fund choices, and have seen most of them approximately triple or more in value over the last ten to twelve years. Under certain circumstances, I have invested up to 6 to 7% of my capital in a given mutual fund at one time. If you are not comfortable with these amounts, either risk lower percentages or stick mostly to mutual funds.

As a disclosure, tracking and acting on insider buying can lead to temporary, or, in some cases, permanent loss of part of your capital (a realized loss). You should be able to financially and emotionally withstand such events should they occur if, or until, your other holdings or the selection recovers. In the 12 years I have practiced this method, I have done very well, growing my assets over time, and maintaining the bulk of my portfolio during the recent turn of the century bear market.

John R. Reizner

Conclusion

Fallibility is, as we all know, all very human. There is no exception to this axiom in the investment world. Emotions often get in the way of fact finding and judgment, and one must often learn to go against the fears we feel. I recall before I purchased Wells Fargo, despite the research ammunition, feeling fear in my belly. After all, my money was at stake. So I just resolved and steeled myself and made the investment. The same is true for my investment in Johnson & Johnson shares, where the political environment was highly unfavorable. There are always events out there that dissuade contrarian-style stock selections, so you should get in the habit of not being led around by your emotions as you invest in the manner described herein.

There is also something to be said about being at the helm of your own financial ship, rather than taking advice from Wall Street. This is both liberating and empowering. After all, stock investment is a worthy calling.

Appendix

Reproductions of the "Guide to Using Daily Graphs" and the "Explanation of the Functional and Technical Features of Daily Graphs" can be found on the following two pages.

Please note on page 28, I have circled item #34, which corresponds to the symbols for insider selling and buying of the sample equity in the legend. The explanations of such buying/selling denoted by these symbols are on page 29, item #34. These are the terms for insider buying and selling to which I refer in this volume.

The examples in the remainder of the appendix are true to life examples taken from past print editions of *Daily Graphs*. I actually invested in many of these stocks. Please study these examples along with my written comments to see a demonstration of the method in action. Also, please refer to the chapter titled "My Insider Buying Rules" as a reference to the examples in order to train yourself in the technique.

GUIDE TO USING DAILY GRAPHS

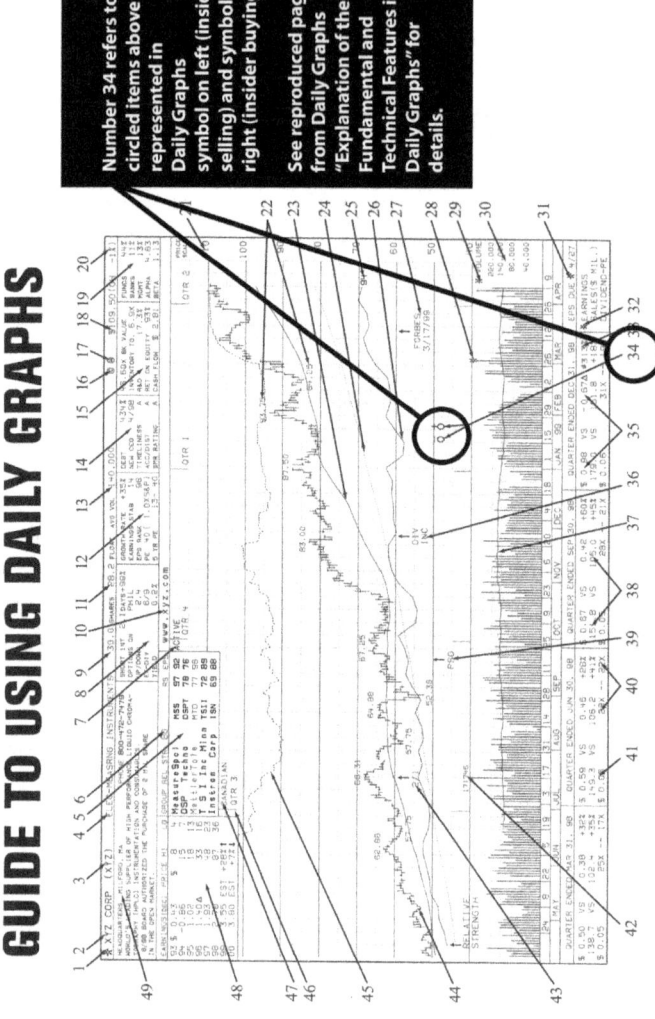

Number 34 refers to circled items above represented in Daily Graphs symbol on left (insider selling) and symbol on right (insider buying).

See reproduced page from Daily Graphs "Explanation of the Fundamental and Technical Features in Daily Graphs" for details.

Reprinted with Permission

John R. Reizner

EXPLANATION OF THE FUNDAMENTAL AND TECHNICAL FEATURES OF DAILY GRAPHS

1. INDICATES... 5-YEAR EARNINGS GROWTH RATE GREATER THAN 20% PER YEAR. (See 12A)

2. COMPANY NAME shown may not necessarily be the exact corporate title due to space limitations.

3. TICKER OR TRADING SYMBOL.

4. INDUSTRY GROUP CLASSIFICATION - Daily Graphs has developed its own group classification of 197 industry groups. Group classification is based on the major source of the company's earnings.

5. THE FIVE STOCKS in the same industry group possessing the highest relative strength (excluding stocks under $10 or trading less than 1,000 shares daily) - The ticker or trading symbol and the Earnings Per Share Rating (EPS) are also given. (Relative Strength Rating is defined in #26.) Bold type indicates stock is listed in a different edition of Daily Graphs.

6. INDUSTRY GROUP RELATIVE STRENGTH - A proprietary formula based on the 6-month price performance of the highest relative strength stocks and the industry group. The highest relative strength stocks account for 75% of the rating. The group performance accounts for 25% of the rating. Industry groups are ranked with a value of 99 (highest) to 1. There are 197 industry groups.

7. ACTIVE (NASDAQ stocks only) indicates one of the 250 highest dollar market value stocks, based on price performance shares outstanding.

8. SHORT INTEREST (REPORTED MONTHLY) indicates the number of days it would take to cover short interest based on the average daily volume. This percentage may increase or decrease from the prior month as also shown.

9. UP/DOWN VOLUME is a ratio of daily up-volume to daily down-volume. This 50-day ratio is derived by dividing the total volume on days when the stock closed up from the previous day by total volume on days it closed down. A ratio greater than 1.0 implies a positive demand.

10. COMMON SHARES OUTSTANDING (IN MILLIONS)

11. FLOATING SUPPLY (IN MILLIONS) - Number of shares available for trading that are not closely held. If no figure appears, all shares are considered to be floating.

12. DATAGLOCK CONTAINING THE FOLLOWING INFORMATION:
    A. FIVE-YEAR EARNINGS GROWTH RATE is calculated using the least squares deviation of 3 to 5 years of earnings per share on a trailing 12-month basis.
    B. EARNINGS STABILITY FACTOR, in percentage form, indicates the deviation of the variability around the trend line fitted through 3 to 5 years of earnings. The lower the number, the more stable the company's earnings history.
    C. EARNINGS PER SHARE RATING (EPS RATING) - A proprietary formula that calculates the percentage change in the last two quarters' earnings versus the same quarters a year earlier, as well as the 5-year growth rate and earnings stability. They are appropriately rated and weighted. The result is compared to the stock for the entire database, listed with a value of 99 (highest) to 1. An EPS rating of 90 means the company produced earnings greater than 90 percent of all companies in the database.
    D. CURRENT PRICE/EARNINGS RATIO is computed weekly using Friday's closing price and the latest trailing 12 months of earnings. CURRENT PRICE/EARNINGS RATIO RELATIVE TO THE S&P 500 P/E RATIO - 1.5 X means the stock's P/E over the last 50 trading days and dividing by 200.

13. AVERAGE DAILY VOLUME indicates the average number of shares traded each day over the last 50 trading days.

14. DATABLOCK CONTAINING THE FOLLOWING INFORMATION:
    A. DEBT PERCENTAGE is calculated using fiscal year-end values and dividing the long-term debt including lease obligations, convertible debt, and mortgages by the total number of shares outstanding.
    B. NEW CEO - A new Chief Executive Officer was appointed in the last two years. Date shown is when appointment was effective.

15. DATABLOCK CONTAINING THE FOLLOWING INFORMATION:
    A. STOCK PRICE RELATIVE TO BOOK VALUE is calculated by dividing the current price by the per share book value (total shareholder's equity for the fiscal year-end divided by common shares outstanding).
    B. SMR RATING (Sales+Profit Margins+Return on Equity) - A company's sales growth rate over the last three quarters, before-and-after-tax profit margins, and Return on Equity. These factors are compared to the rest of times inventory has turned over in the last fiscal year (total revenue divided by average of beginning and ending inventory) based on liquid year-end values.
    C. RESEARCH AND DEVELOPMENT is the percent of total sales spent on research and development in the last fiscal year.
    D. RETURN ON EQUITY PERCENTAGE is computed by dividing annual income (before extraordinary items, cumulative effects and discontinued operations) adjustments and non-recurring items) by an average of the latest fiscal year and the prior year's stockholders equity.
    E. CASH FLOW PER SHARE from OPERATIONS is derived by adding the depreciation, depletion and amortization to the company's net income and dividing this figure by the shares outstanding.

16. INDICATES THE COMPANY HAS CONVERTIBLE ISSUES (BONDS OR PREFERREDS)

17. INDICATES THE COMPANY HAS WARRANTS OUTSTANDING

18. CLOSING PRICE is the last trade of the week on a composite basis as transacted on all exchanges.

19. DATABLOCK CONTAINING THE FOLLOWING INFORMATION:
    A. MUTUAL FUND SPONSORSHIP is the percentage of floating supply of stock owned by mutual funds as reported quarterly.
    B. BANK SPONSORSHIP is the percentage of floating supply of stock reported quarterly by approximately 750 banks.
    C. MANAGEMENT % is the percentage of outstanding shares held by management.
    D. ALPHA measures how much the stock would have fluctuated on average every month over the past 12 months, assuming the S&P 500 Index was unchanged during the period. For example, an Alpha of 1.0 means the stock's price would have appreciated or unchanged (assuming the S&P 500 Index during 12 months, assuming an unchanged S&P 500 Index. Alpha is calculated weekly.
    E. BETA measures the stock's sensitivity to movement in the S&P 500 Index over a 12-month period. A Beta of 1.50 suggests a stock tends to be 50% more volatile than the S&P 500 Index. Beta is calculated weekly.

20. PERCENTAGE STOCK'S CLOSING PRICE IS BELOW ITS HIGH PRICE DURING THE LAST 12 MONTHS.

21. ARITHMETIC PRICE SCALE

22. HIGHLIGHTS EXACT PRICES AT KEY HIGH OR LOW POINTS

23. 50-DAY MOVING AVERAGE PRICE LINE is calculated by adding the closing price over the last 50 trading days and dividing by 50.

24. 200-DAY MOVING AVERAGE PRICE LINE is calculated by adding the closing price over the last 200 trading days and dividing by 200.

25. RELATIVE STRENGTH RATING is the result of calculating the percentage price changes of the stock over the last 12 months with more weight (40%) assigned to the most recent 3 months and less weight to the prior 9 months. All stocks are arranged in order of price change and ranked with a value of 99 (highest) to 1. A relative strength rating of 99 means the stock has outperformed 99% of all stocks in the database.

26. RELATIVE STRENGTH (COMPARED TO THE S&P 500 INDEX is plotted on a weekly basis. The line is derived by dividing the stock price by the S&P 500 Index value. The scale is determined by the price itself. When the stock's relative strength line is rising, the stock's price performance is better than the S&P 500 Index. A scale is not applicable.

27. ARTICLE IN A MAJOR PUBLICATION - Article on the company or its stock (including date of publication) that appears in Fortune, Business Week, Forbes, Electronic Business, Barron's, etc.

28. INDICATES THE WEEKLY VOLUME WAS THE 2ND HIGHEST IN THE LAST 12 MONTHS.

29. INDICATES THE STOCK MET ONE OF THE FOLLOWING CRITERIA LAST WEEK: (a) volume was at the highest level in the last 52 weeks, (b) volume was at least 100% greater than its average daily volume.

30. STOCKS VOLUME SCALE (Logarithmic; MARKET AVERAGE SCALE is arithmetic.

31. INDICATES EARNINGS ARE EXPECTED TO BE REPORTED WITHIN THE NEXT 4 WEEKS - Anticipated date is also shown.

32. INDICATES EARNINGS WERE REPORTED IN THE LAST TWO WEEKS

33. PREVIOUS YEAR - A # denotes comparison quarter was negative.

34. INSIDER BUYING/SELLING - Single bubbles which equal or multiple trades which aggregate 100 shares or more, will generate an insider Buy (B or matter sell (S) appearing in the week it was transacted. Traders generated due to stock dividends, splits or simple sales or acquisition are not included.

35. DIVIDEND - Company announced a change in the quarterly payout. Dimensions shown in cents is the quarterly rate.

36. DIVIDEND - Company announced a change in the quarterly payout. Dimensions shown in cents is the quarterly rate.

37. HORIZONTAL LINE indicating the 50-day average daily volumes of the stock. The VOLUME LINE is the day's volume.

38. QUARTERLY SALES COMPARED TO THE SAME QUARTER OF PREVIOUS YEAR - Also shown, the percentage change in sales.

39. STOCK MARKET MOVEMENTS - Tender offer (TO), proposed secondary offering (PSO), secondary offer (SO), proposed merger (PM), cash offer (CO), spin-off (SOF), partial spin-off (PSOF), stock (RECPSO), initial public offering (IPO), new issue and price (NEW), (ASE) indicates the date the stock was switched to a listed Exchange.

40. HIGH AND LOW PRICE/EARNINGS RATIO FOR THE QUARTER

41. CASH DIVIDEND FOR THE QUARTER

42. VOLUME PEAKS (IN HUNDREDS) - Volume lines above the scale have been truncated to fit the stock graph and the actual volume figure is given.

43. STOCK DIVIDEND OR SPLIT - Prior prices, earnings and volume are adjusted at the time of either a stock dividend or split.

44. DAILY COMPOSITE HIGH, LOW AND CLOSING PRICES - Closing price is indicated with a tick.

45. TICKER TAPE VOLUME LINE is the result of adding the volume of all up-trades and subtracting the volume of all down-trades for each trading day. A sequence of up-trades (an uptick) and down-trades (a downtick) can be identified as unusually high priced trades. As this is a cumulative value, a scale is not applicable; only the slope of the line is of value. (When the slope is positive, more shares are being traded on upticks.)

46. VERTICAL LINES INDICATE BEGINNING OF THE CALENDAR QUARTER

47. INDICATES THE COMPANY FINANCIALS (EARNINGS AND SALES, ETC.) are in Canadian dollars.

48. DATABLOCK CONTAINING THE FOLLOWING INFORMATION:
    A. FISCAL YEAR-END is denoted by placing month in parentheses to the right of EARNINGS.
    B. SIX-YEAR RECORD OF ANNUAL OPERATING EARNINGS - A delta (a) to the right of EPS denotes fiscal year was restated.
    C. CALENDAR YEAR HIGH/LOW PRICES FOR PAST SIX YEARS (adjusted for all stock dividends and splits)
    D. EARNINGS PER SHARE ESTIMATE - Composite of the 3 most current "latest" estimates for the fiscal year and following years (when available)
    E. PERCENTAGE INCREASE/DECREASE IN EARNINGS ESTIMATES COMPARED TO THE PRIOR YEAR
    F. ESTIMATE REVISION - Indicates earnings estimates were revised last week and were above (1) or below (4) our previously published consensus earnings estimate.

49. BUSINESS SUMMARY is a brief description of the company's business operations including recent corporate developments. The headquarters's location and telephone number are shown.

JP Morgan Chase & Co: June 2002 - May 2003

→ Investment while stock is under pressure.

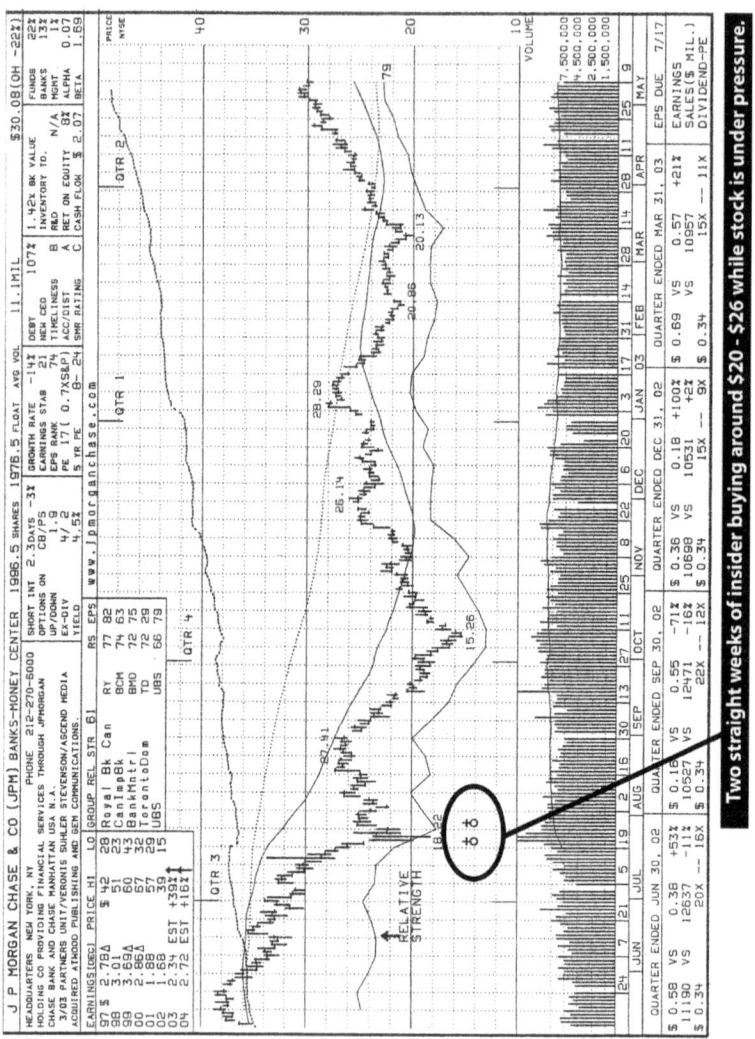

Reprinted with Permission

John R. Reizner

JP Morgan Chase & Co: May 2003 - April 2004

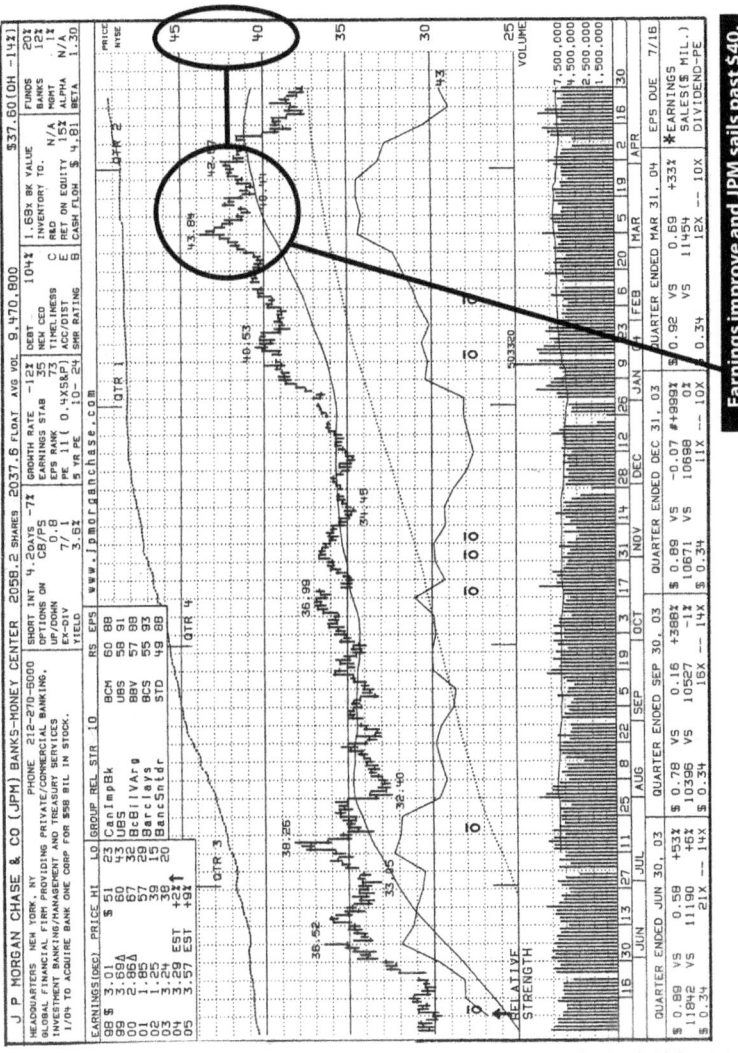

Sears: June 2002 - May 2003

→ With many companies, an abrupt decline such as this would not be reversed upwardly. It takes time to see if the company's stock price will continue declining or stabilize over time and move upward.

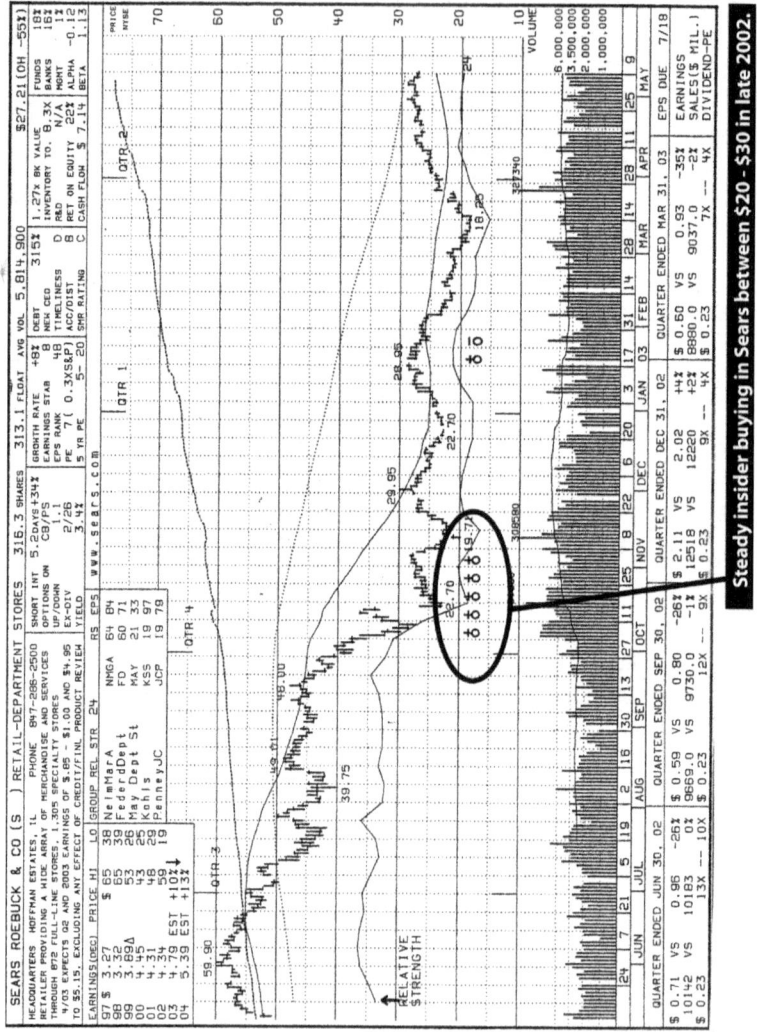

Reprinted with Permission

John R. Reizner

Sears: May 2003 - April 2004

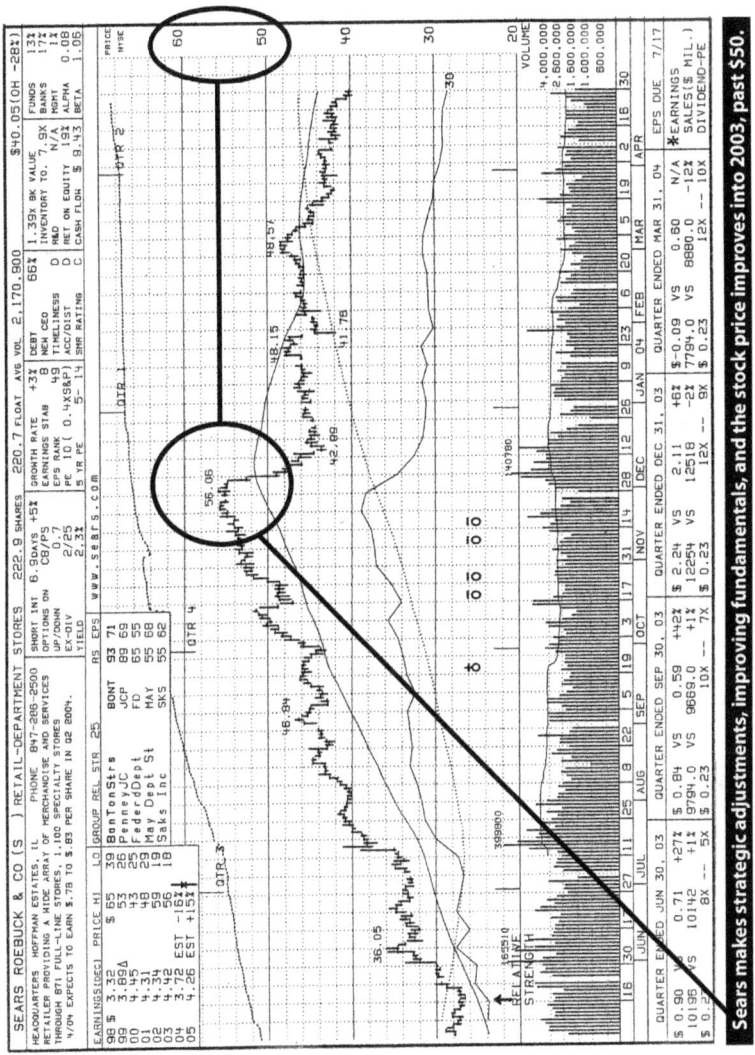

Reprinted with Permission

Deluxe Corp: September 2000 - August 2001

→ Investment during a general Bear Market.

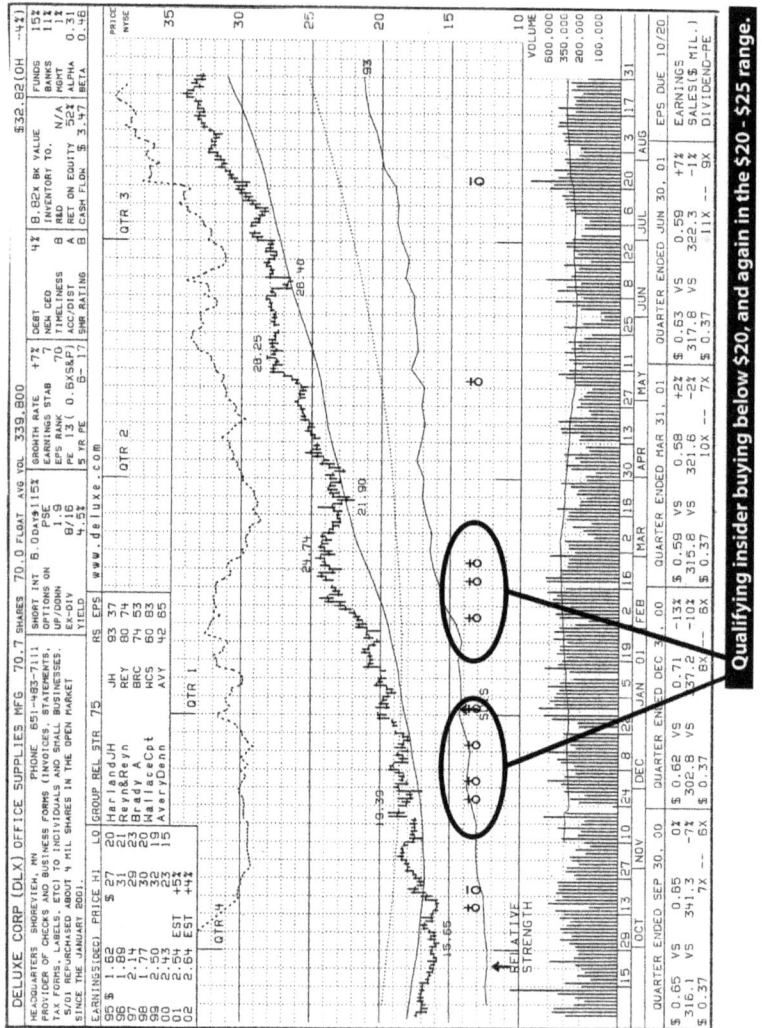

John R. Reizner

Deluxe Corp: August 2001 - August 2002

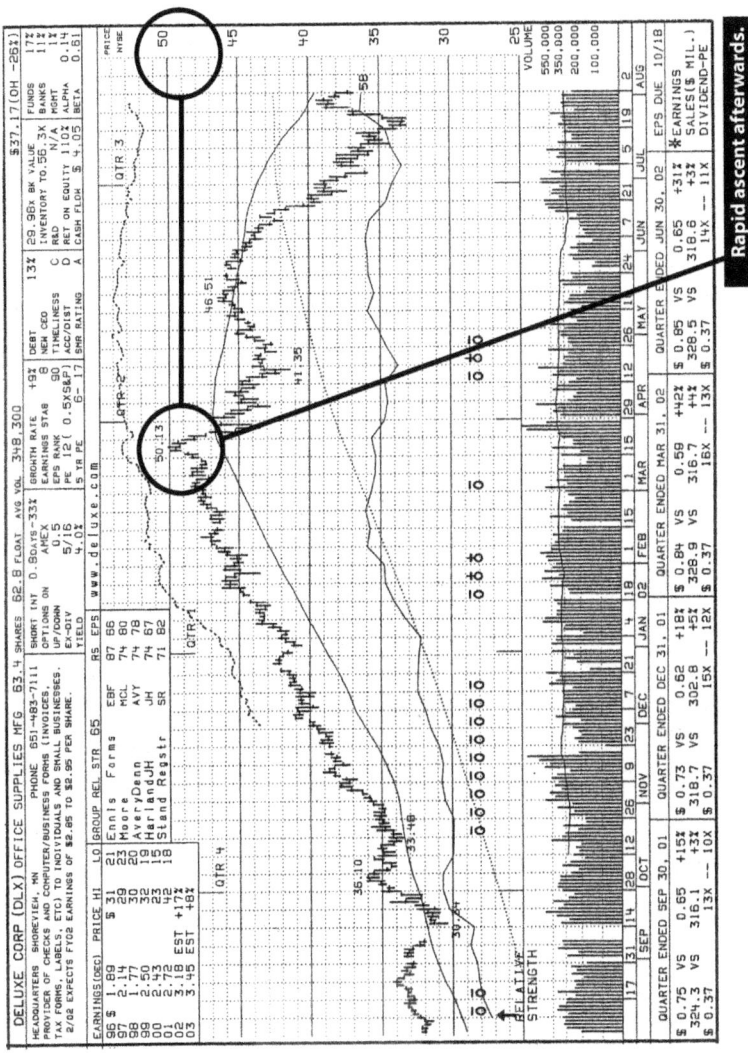

Reprinted with Permission

Family Dollar Stores: June 1999 - May 2000

→ In 1999, buying near a general market top: a success story.

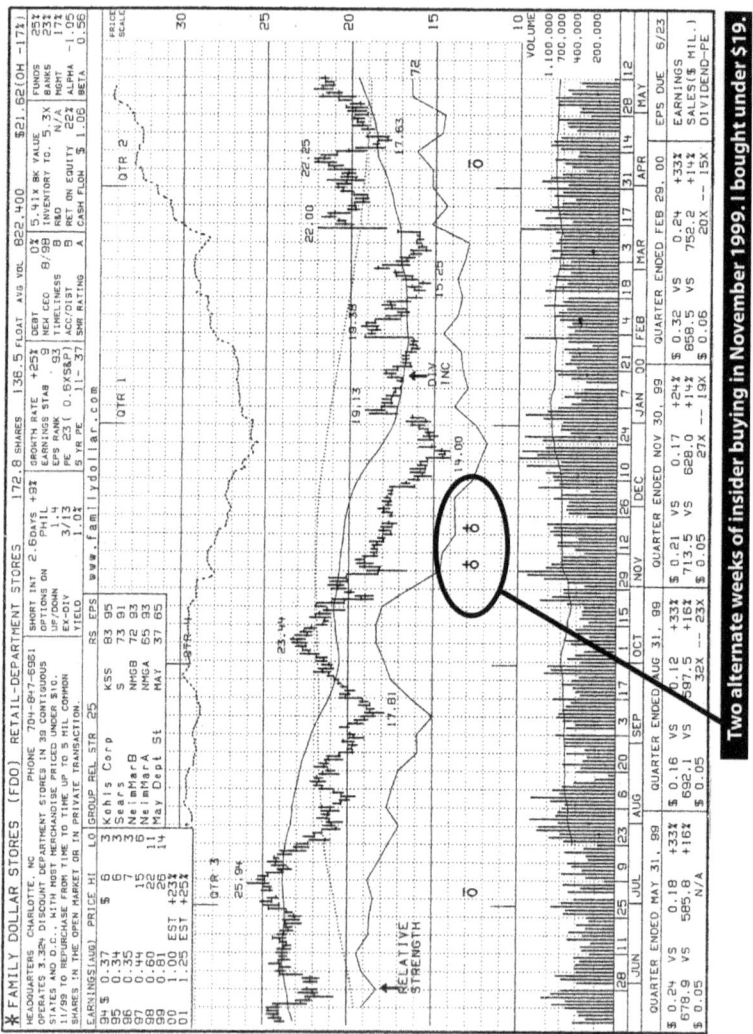

Reprinted with Permission

Family Dollar Stores: September 2000 - August 2001

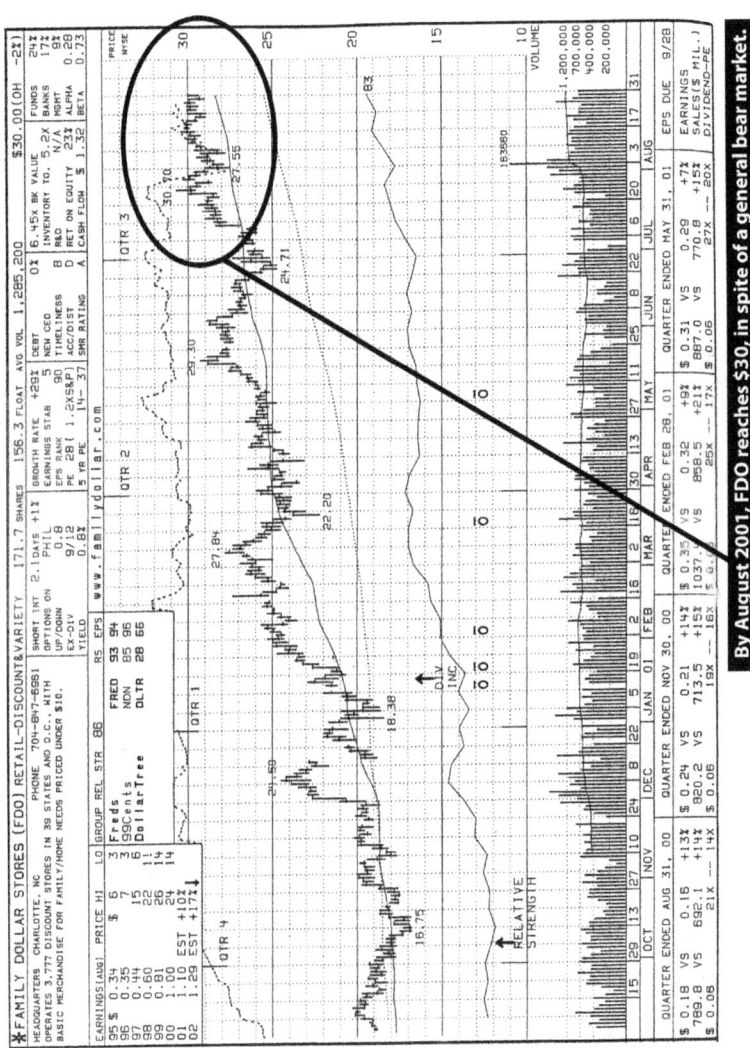

Reprinted with Permission

Tenet Healthcare: June 1999 - May 2000

→ Investment after stock decline.

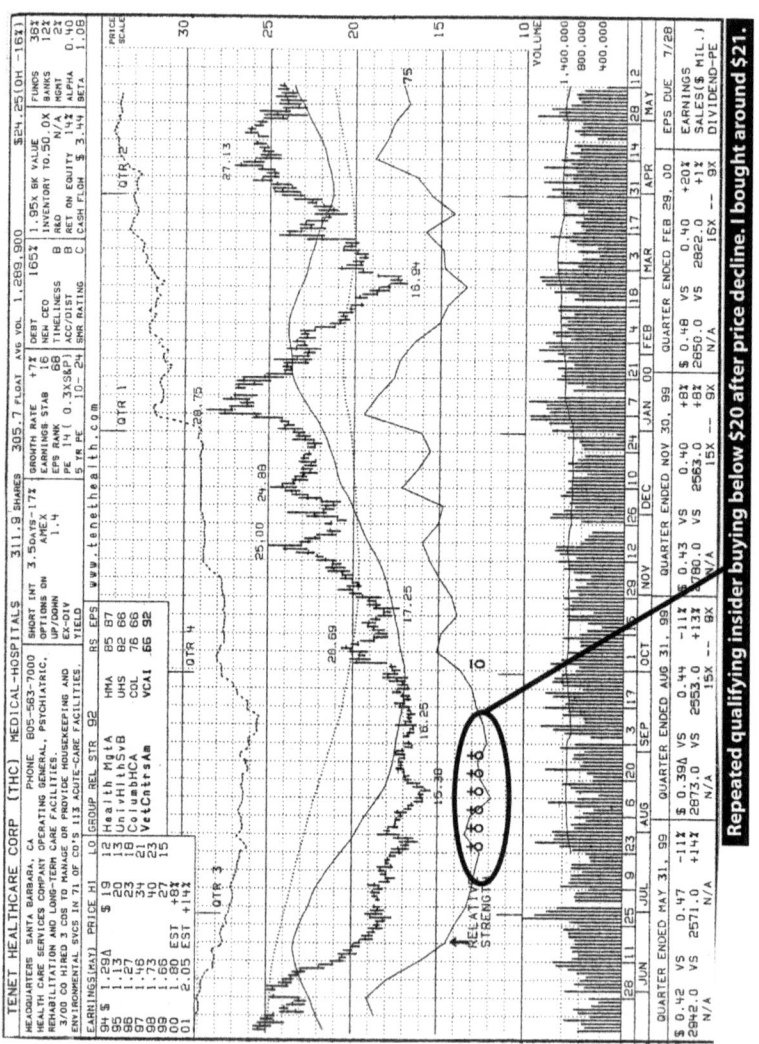

John R. Reizner

Tenet Healthcare: September 2000 - August 2001

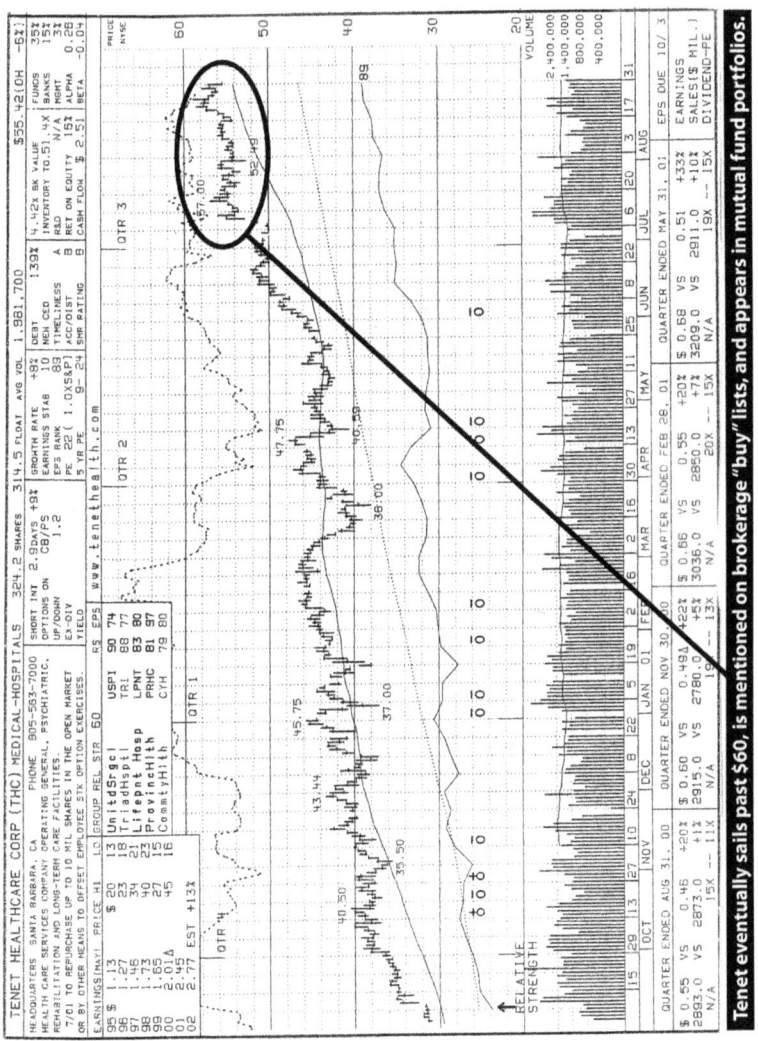

Reprinted with Permission

Hilton Hotels Corp: December 1983 - December 1984

→ Hilton corrects in the first general market correction of the
   Great 1980's Bull Market.

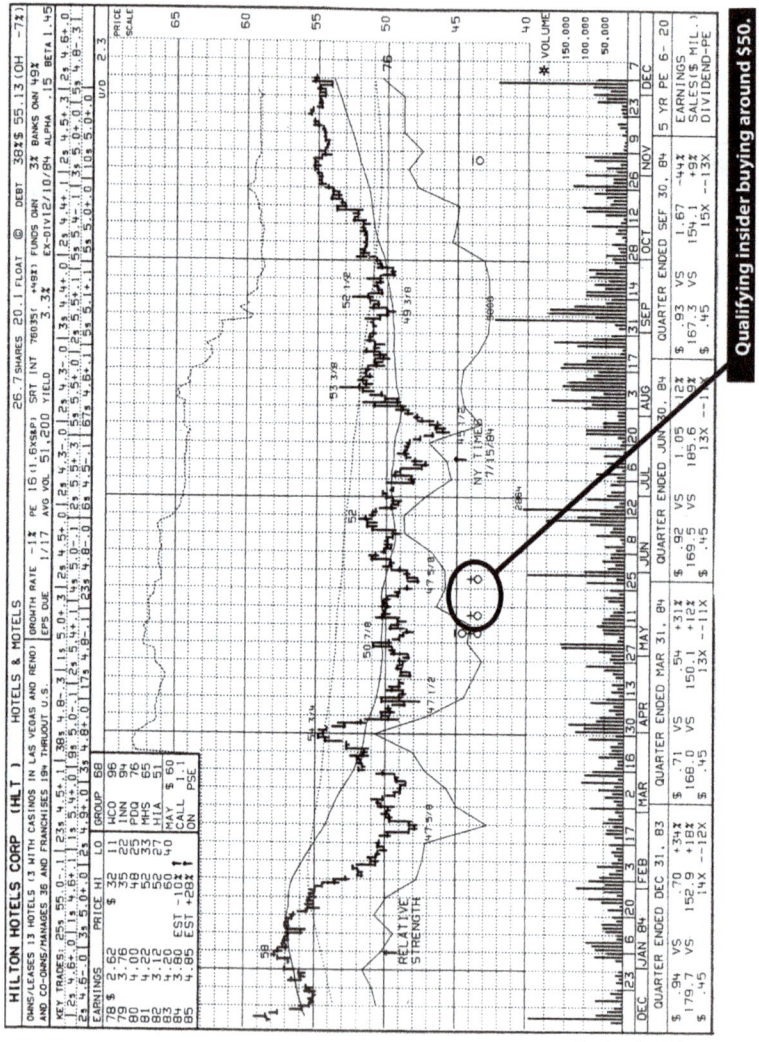

Qualifying insider buying around $50.

Reprinted with Permission

John R. Reizner

Hilton Hotels Corp: September 1985 - September 1986

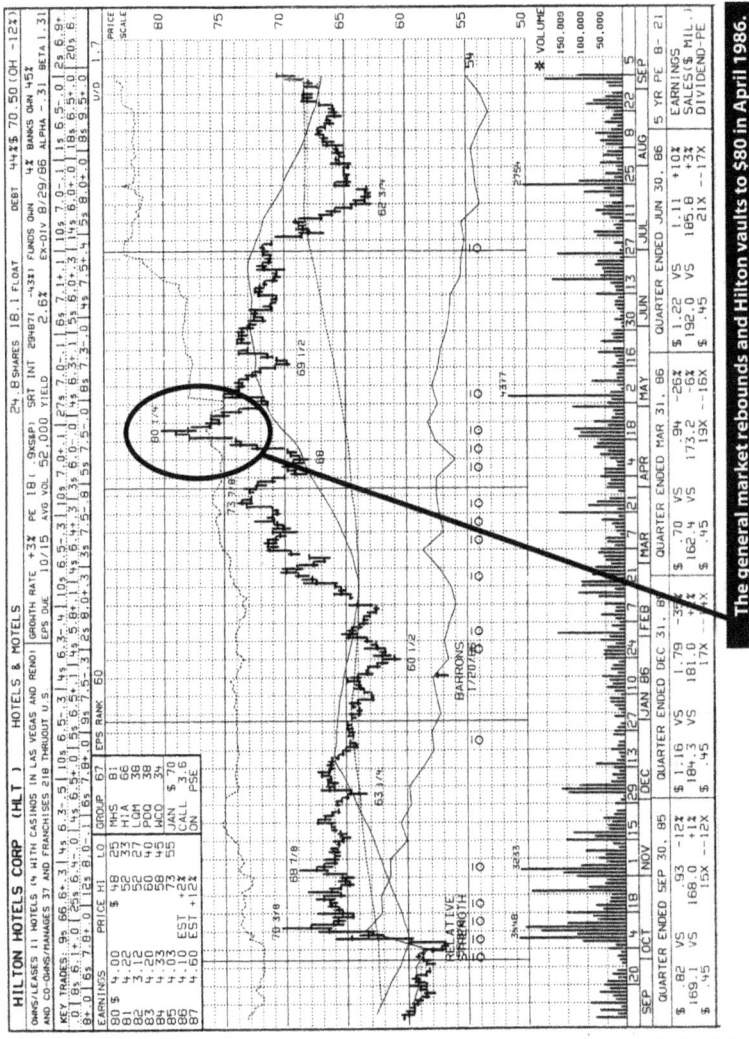

Reprinted with Permission

Federal Express: January 1984 - December 1984

→ Buying Federal Express during a general market correction in 1984.

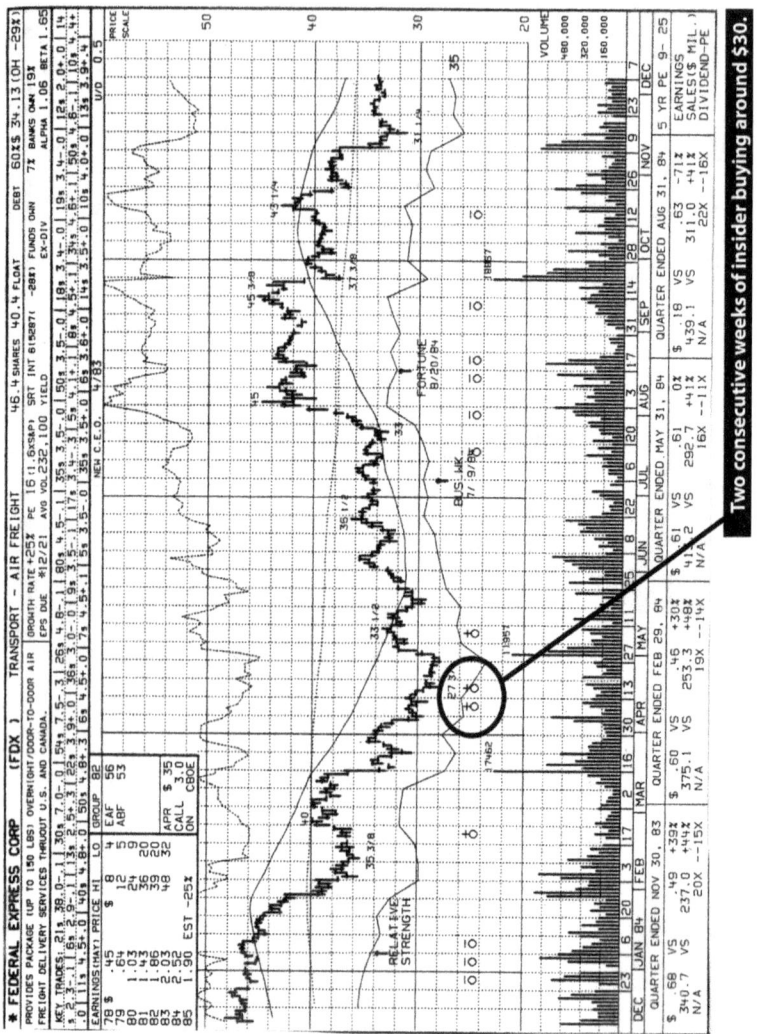

John R. Reizner

Federal Express: September 1985 - September 1986

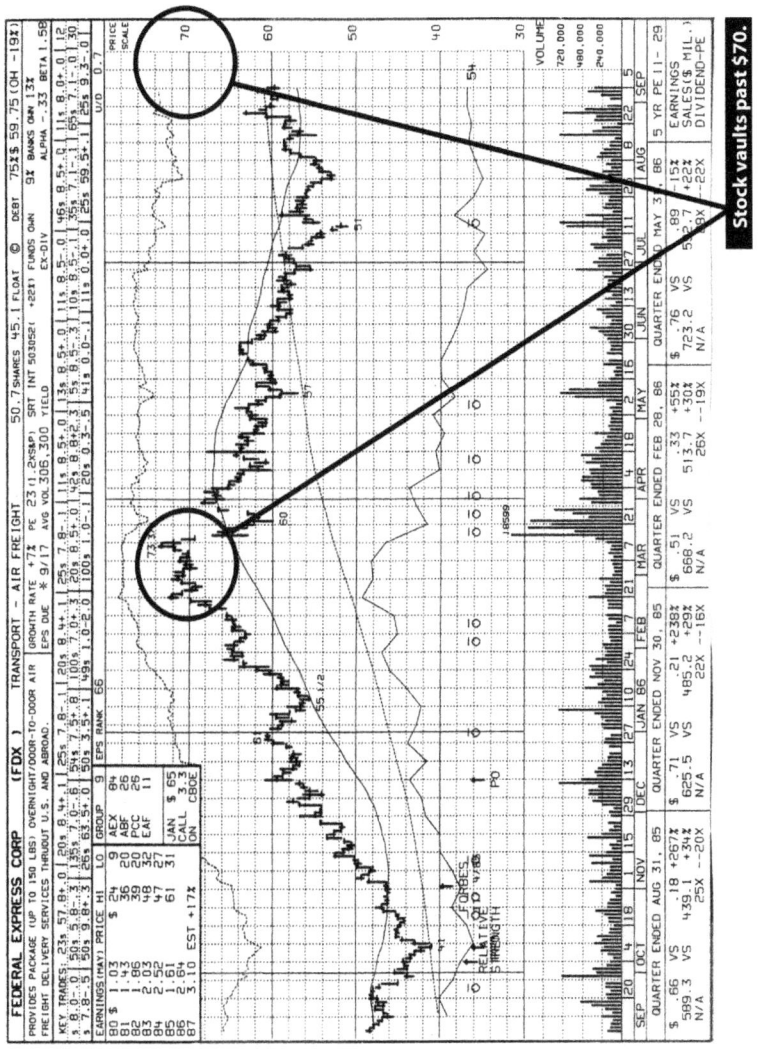

Reprinted with Permission

Georgia Pacific Corp: January 1984 - December 1984

→ In 1984, commodity company shows insider buying.

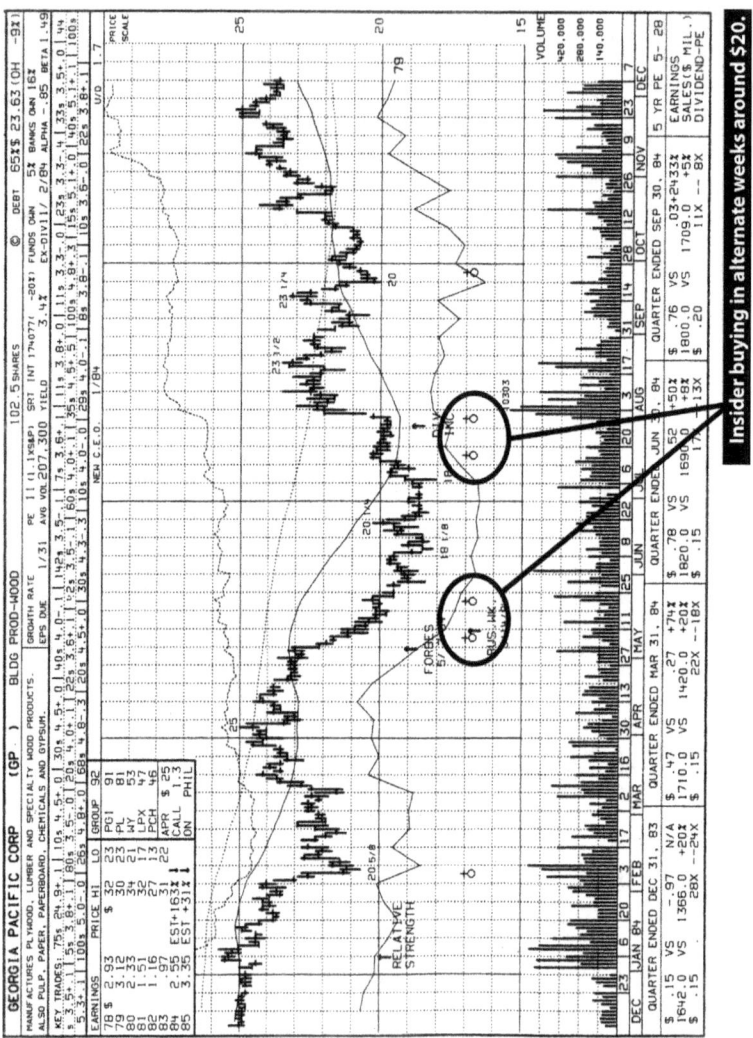

Reprinted with Permission

John R. Reizner

Georgia Pacific Corp: September 1985 - September 1986

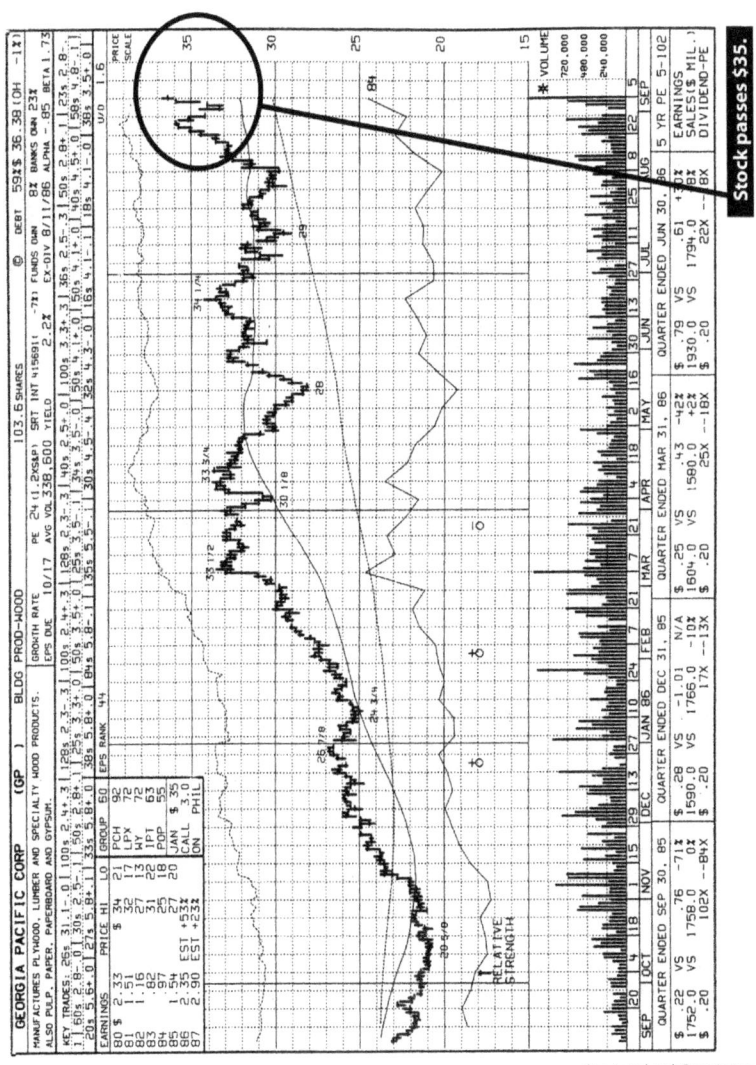

Reprinted with Permission

Morton Thiokol: January 1984 - December 1984

→ Buying Morton Thiokol during a general market correction in 1984.

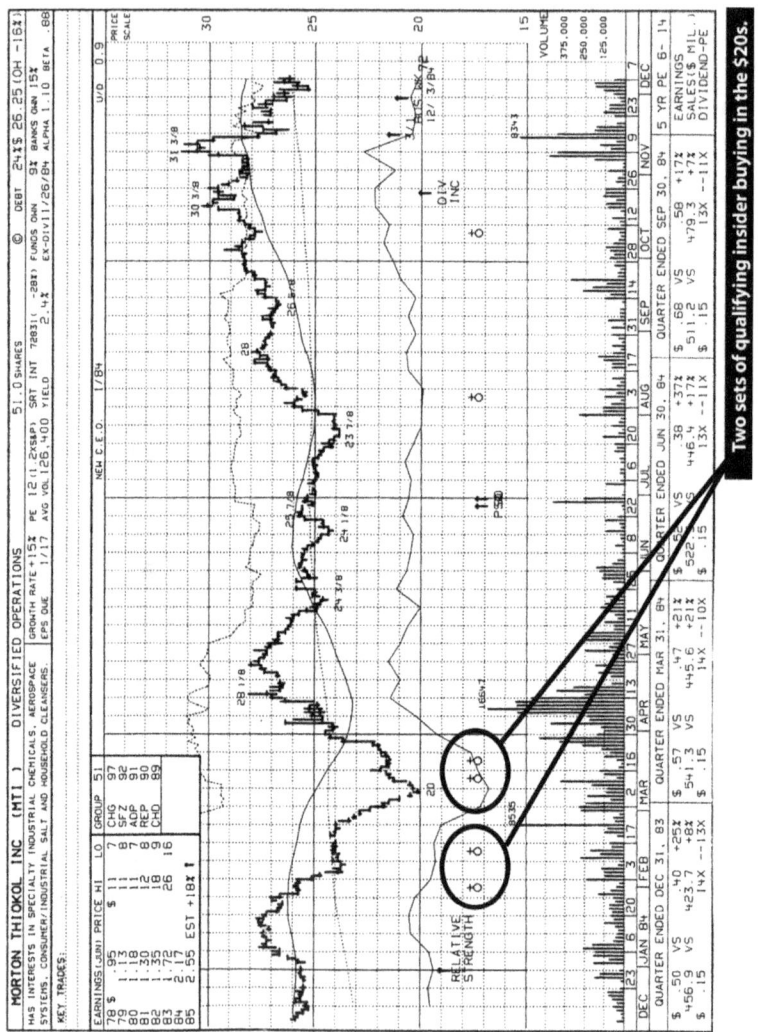

Reprinted with Permission

Morton Thiokol: July 1984 - July 1985

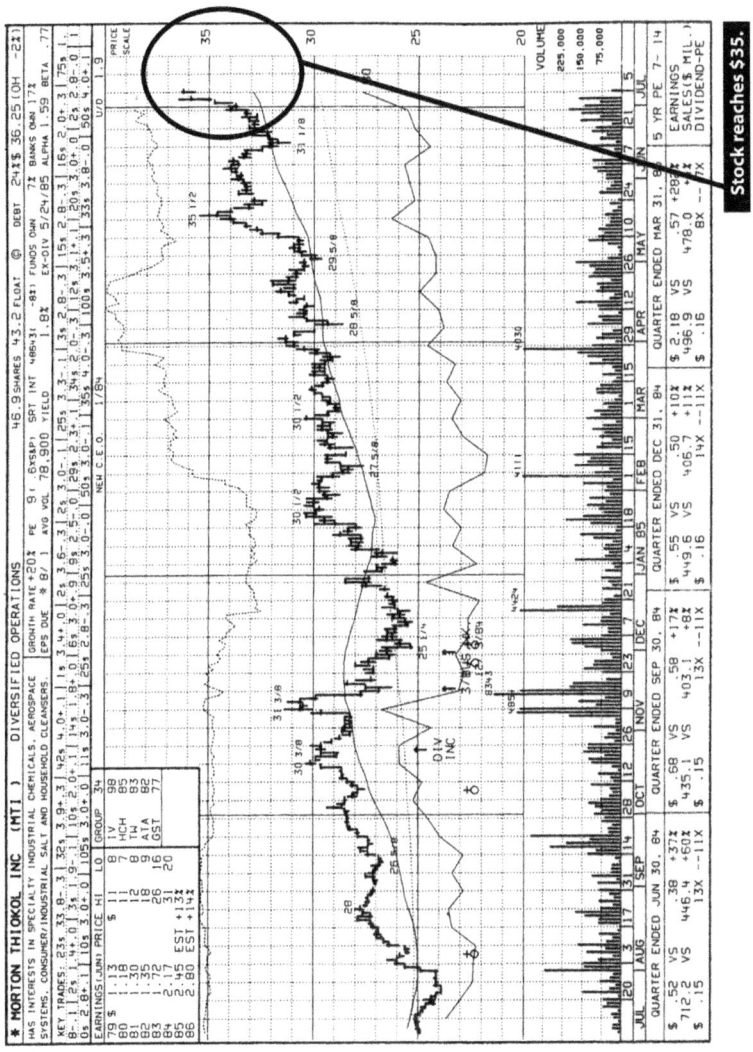

Reprinted with Permission

Exxon Corp: December 1983 - December 1984

→ Buying a major oil company that shows insider buying that meets my rules.

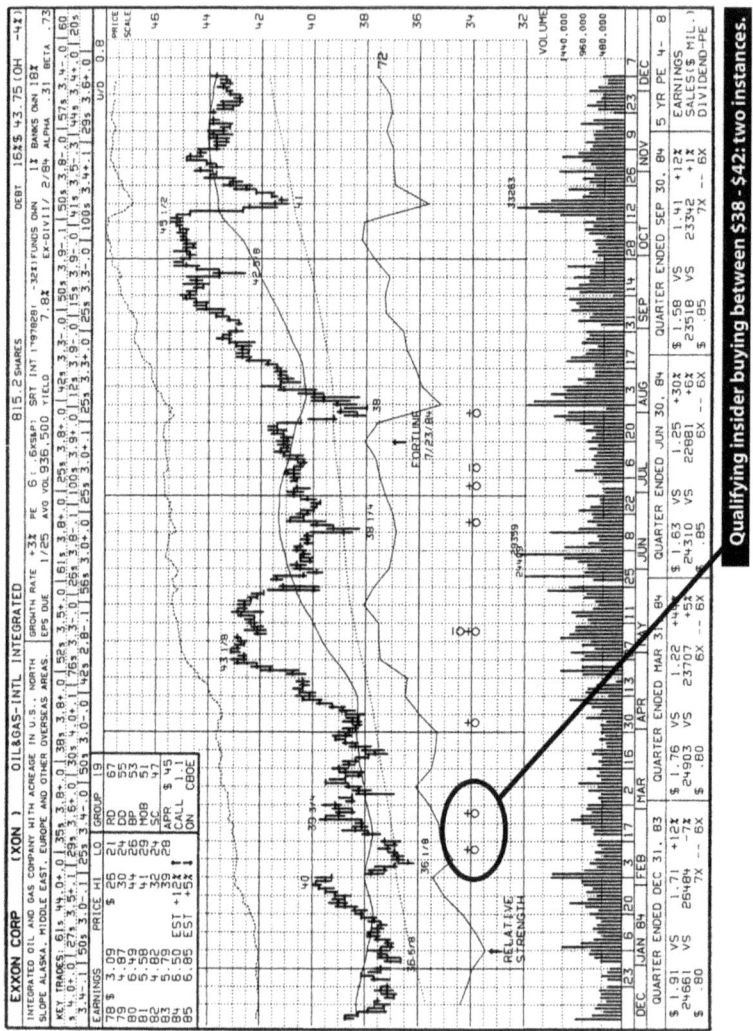

Reprinted with Permission

John R. Reizner

Exxon Corp: September 1985 - September 1986

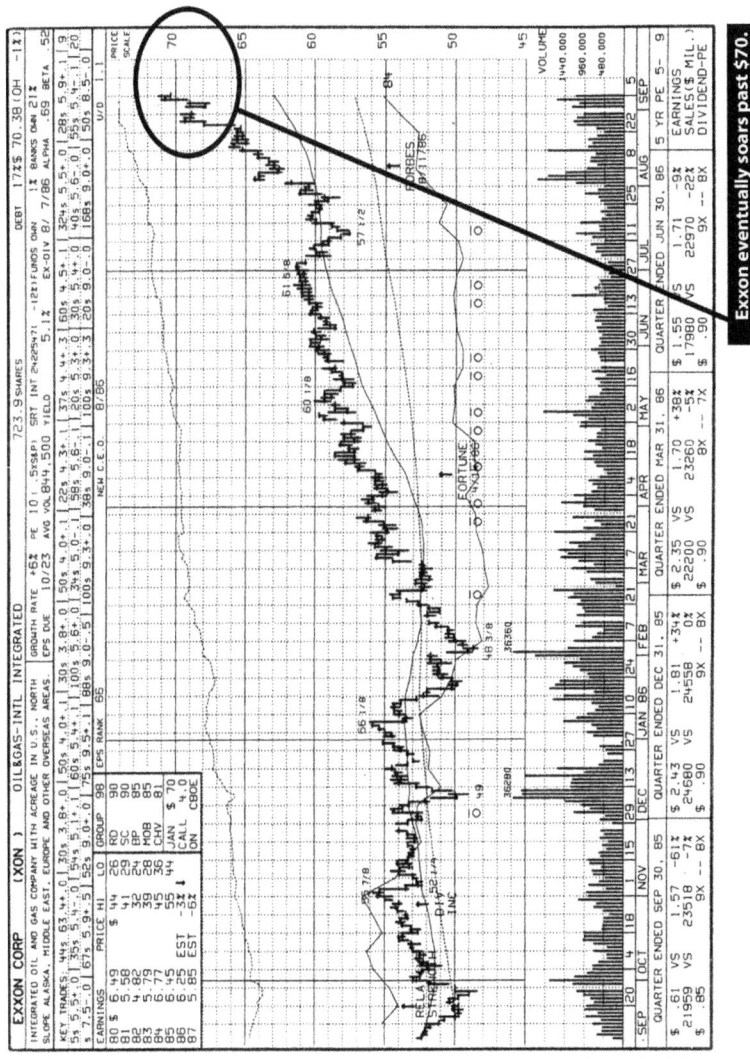

Reprinted with Permission

Textron: January 1982 - January 1984

→ 1980's bull era example of steady insider buying that qualifys under the rules.

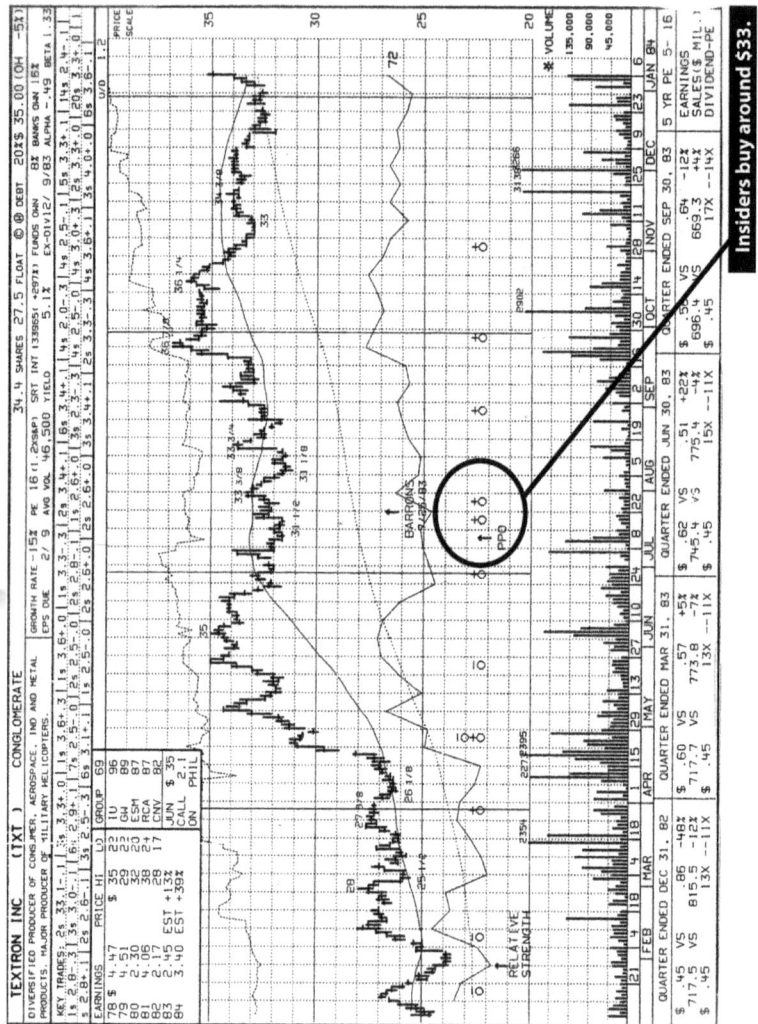

Reprinted with Permission

Textron: December 1984 - December 1985

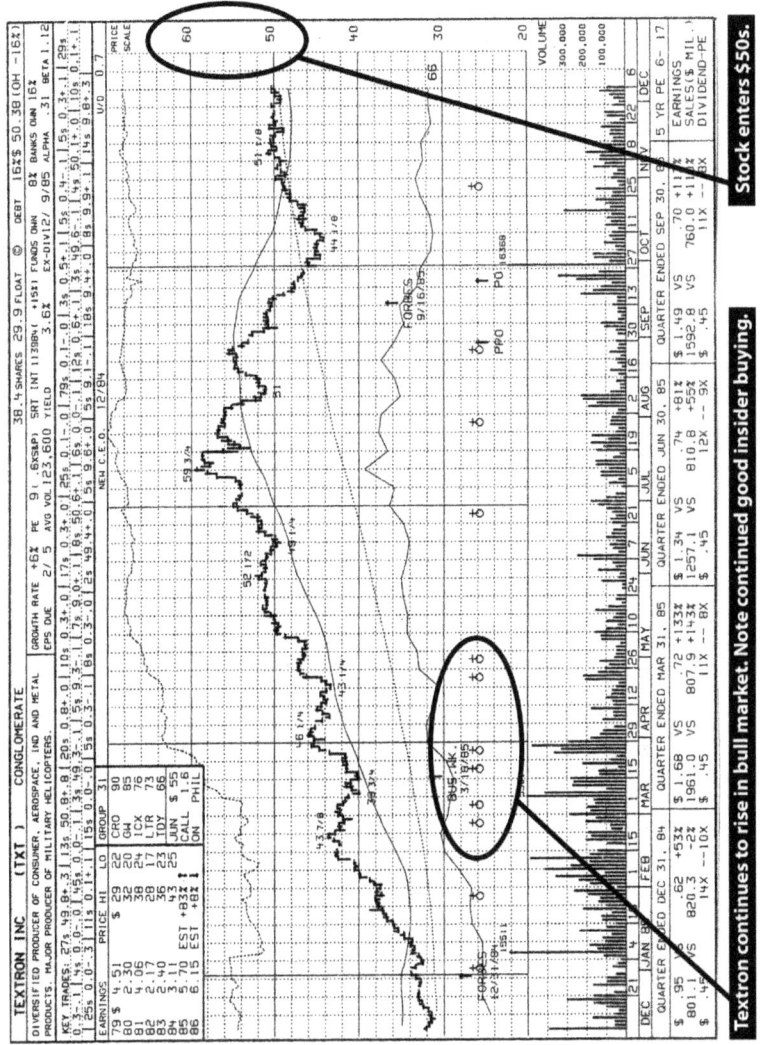

Reprinted with Permission

www.ingramcontent.com/pod-product-compliance
Lightning Source LLC
Chambersburg PA
CBHW051244170526
45165CB00004B/1565